GW01191692

James McNeill Whistler

A BOOK OF POSTCARDS

FREER GALLERY OF ART   SMITHSONIAN INSTITUTION

Pomegranate Artbooks, San Francisco

Pomegranate Artbooks
Box 808022
Petaluma, CA 94975

ISBN 1-56640-441-X
Pomegranate Catalog No. A648

Pomegranate also publishes over sixty other postcard collections on different subjects.
Please write to the publisher for more information.

The American-born artist James McNeill Whistler (1834–1903) left the United States at the age of twenty-one and never returned to his native country. He began his expatriate life as a student in Paris but eventually settled in London. During the 1860s, as he attempted to discard the realist style he had adopted in France, Whistler found inspiration in Japanese prints and Chinese porcelain. By the 1870s he was transforming scenes of contemporary life, especially along the banks of the River Thames, into tranquil views of the city, veiled in mood and atmosphere. He gave his works musical titles and incorporated elements of Japanese style into his compositions. His monogram, which took the form of a butterfly, served as a signature on many of his paintings. Whistler's works were regarded as eccentric during his lifetime, but today they are considered among the most innovative and original of the nineteenth century.

The Freer Gallery of Art in Washington, D.C., contains over twelve hundred paintings, prints and drawings by Whistler. This remarkable collection, the most extensive in the world, was largely the result of Whistler's friendship with the museum's founder, Charles Lang Freer (1854–1919). In 1906, Freer presented his Whistler holdings to the nation, together with paintings by a select group of American artists active around the turn of the century and an outstanding collection of Asian art. Although he stipulated that no further additions be made to his American holdings, Freer did permit acquisitions in other areas. Consequently, since the Freer Gallery opened to the public in 1923, the museum has assembled a preeminent collection of Asian Art, while continuing to honor the founder's commitment to the exhibition of American works.

The thirty paintings reproduced in this book of postcards represent some of Whistler's most outstanding works from the Freer's extensive collection.

James McNeill Whistler (1834–1903)

Annabel Lee, c. 1870
Pastel on brown paper
32.5 x 18.0 cm (12¾ x 7¹⁄₁₆ in.), 05.129

Pomegranate, Box 808022, Petaluma, CA 94975

Freer Gallery of Art, Smithsonian Institution

James McNeill Whistler (1834–1903)

Pink Note: The Novelette, early 1880s
Watercolor
25.3 x 15.5 cm (10 x 6⅛ in.), 02.158

Pomegranate, Box 808022, Petaluma, CA 94975

James McNeill Whistler (1834–1903)

Variations in Flesh Colour and Green: The Balcony,
1864–1870
Oil on panel
61.4 x 48.8 cm (24⅛ x 19¼ in.), 92.23

Pomegranate, Box 808022, Petaluma, CA 94975

James McNeill Whistler (1834–1903)

Southend Pier, 1880s
Watercolor
18.2 x 25.7 cm (7⅛ x 10⅛ in.), 04.82

Pomegranate, Box 808022, Petaluma, CA 94975

Freer Gallery of Art, Smithsonian Institution

James McNeill Whistler (1834–1903)

Rose and Silver: Portrait of Mrs. Whibley,
early 1890s
Watercolor
28.2 x 18.8 cm (11⅛ x 7⅜ in.), 01.108

Pomegranate, Box 808022, Petaluma, CA 94975

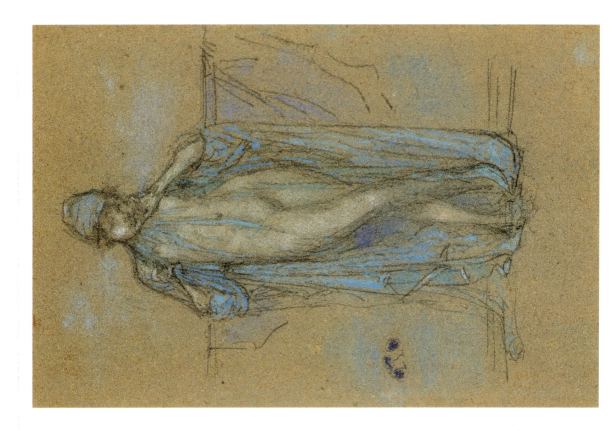

James McNeill Whistler (1834–1903)

Harmony in Blue and Violet, late 1880s
Pastel on brown paper
28.0 x 18.0 cm (11 x 7⅛ in.), 90.8

Pomegranate, Box 808022, Petaluma, CA 94975

James McNeill Whistler (1834–1903)
Southend: The Pleasure Yacht, early 1880s
Watercolor
25.4 x 17.9 cm (10 x 7 in.), 05.120

Pomegranate, Box 808022, Petaluma, CA 94975

James McNeill Whistler (1834–1903)

Note in Pink and Purple: The Studio, early 1880s
Watercolor
30.4 x 22.8 cm (12 x 9 in.), 02.163

Pomegranate, Box 808022, Petaluma, CA 94975

James McNeill Whistler (1834–1903)
Nocturne: Grand Canal, Amsterdam, 1883–1884
Watercolor
22.7 x 28.4 cm (9 x 11⅛ in.), 02.161

Pomegranate, Box 808022, Petaluma, CA 94975

Freer Gallery of Art, Smithsonian Institution

James McNeill Whistler (1834–1903)

Venus Rising from the Sea, c. 1869–1870
Oil on canvas
59.8 x 49.1 cm (23½ x 19¼ in.), 03.174

Pomegranate, Box 808022, Petaluma, CA 94975

James McNeill Whistler (1834–1903)

Breakfast in the Garden, 1880s
Watercolor
12.7 x 21.9 cm (5 x 8½ in.), 05.122

Pomegranate, Box 808022, Petaluma, CA 94975

Freer Gallery of Art, Smithsonian Institution

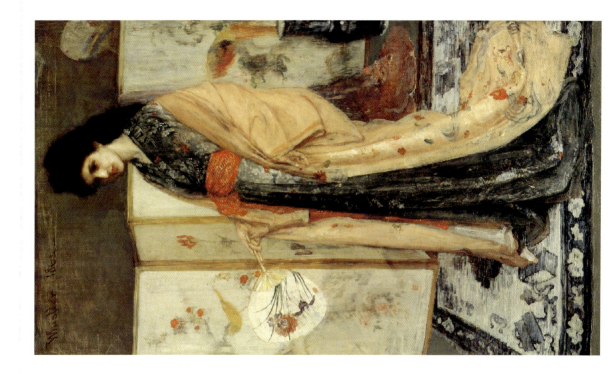

James McNeill Whistler (1834–1903)

La Princesse du pays de la porcelaine, 1863–1864
Oil on canvas
199.9 x 116.1 cm (78¾ x 45¾ in.), 03.91

Pomegranate, Box 808022, Petaluma, CA 94975

Freer Gallery of Art, Smithsonian Institution

James McNeill Whistler (1834–1903)
Variations in Pink and Grey: Chelsea, 1871–1872
Oil on canvas
62.7 x 40.5 cm (24⅝ x 16 in.), 02.249

Pomegranate, Box 808022, Petaluma, CA 94975

James McNeill Whistler (1834–1903)

Harmony in Blue and Gold: The Little Blue Girl,
1894–1903
Oil on canvas
74.7 x 50.5 cm (29⅜ x 19⅞ in.), 03.89

Pomegranate. Box 808022. Petaluma. CA 94975

James McNeill Whistler (1834–1903)

Harmony in Green and Rose: The Music Room,
1860–1861
Oil on canvas
96.3 x 71.7 cm (37¹⁵⁄₁₆ x 28¼ in.), 17.234

Pomegranate, Box 808022, Petaluma, CA 94975

James McNeill Whistler (1834–1903)

Red and Pink: La Petite Mephiste, early 1880s
Oil on composition board mounted on panel
25.4 x 20.3 cm (10 x 8 in.), 02.147

Pomegranate, Box 808022, Petaluma, CA 94975

James McNeill Whistler (1834–1903)
Nocturne: Blue and Gold—Valparaiso, begun 1866
Oil on canvas
75.6 x 50.1 cm (29¾ x 19¾ in.), 09.127

Pomegranate, Box 808022, Petaluma, CA 94975

James McNeill Whistler (1834–1903)

Milly Finch, early 1880s
Watercolor
29.8 x 22.5 cm (11¾ x 8⅞ in.), 07.170

Pomegranate, Box 808022, Petaluma, CA 94975

Freer Gallery of Art, Smithsonian Institution

James McNeill Whistler (1834–1903)
Note in Blue and Opal: The Sun Cloud, 1884
Oil on panel
12.4 x 21.7 cm (4⅞ x 8½ in.), 04.314

Pomegranate, Box 808022, Petaluma, CA 94975

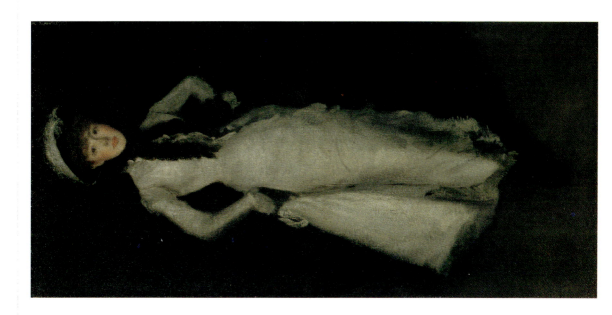

James McNeill Whistler (1834–1903)

Arrangement in White and Black, c. 1873
Oil on canvas
191.4 x 90.9 cm (75⅜ x 35¾ in.), 04.78

Pomegranate, Box 808022, Petaluma, CA 94975

Freer Gallery of Art, Smithsonian Institution

James McNeill Whistler (1834–1903)
Chelsea Shops, mid 1880s
Watercolor
12.5 x 21.0 cm (4^{15}⁄$_{16}$ x 8¼ in.), 04.79

Pomegranate, Box 808022, Petaluma, CA 94975

Freer Gallery of Art, Smithsonian Institution

James McNeill Whistler (1834–1903)

The Little Red Glove 1896–1902
Oil on canvas
51.3 x 31.5 cm (20¼ X 12⅜ in.), 03.180

Pomegranate, Box 808022, Petaluma, CA 94975

Freer Gallery of Art, Smithsonian Institution

James McNeill Whistler (1834–1903)
The Thames in Ice, 1860
Oil on canvas
74.6 x 55.3 cm (29⅜ x 21¾ in.), 01.107

Pomegranate, Box 808022, Petaluma, CA 94975

Freer Gallery of Art, Smithsonian Institution

James McNeill Whistler (1834–1903)

Symphony in Blue and Pink, c. 1868
Oil on millboard mounted on panel
46.7 x 61.8 cm (18⅜ x 24⅜ in.), 03.179

Pomegranate, Box 808022, Petaluma, CA 94975

James McNeill Whistler (1834–1903)

Symphony in Green and Violet, c. 1868
Oil on millboard mounted on panel
61.9 x 45.8 cm (24⅜ x 18 in.), 03.176

Pomegranate, Box 808022, Petaluma, CA 94975

James McNeill Whistler (1834–1903)

Symphony in White and Red, c. 1868
Oil on millboard mounted on panel
46.8 x 61.8 cm (18⅜ x 24⅜ in.), 03.177

Pomegranate, Box 808022, Petaluma, CA 94975

James McNeill Whistler (1834–1903)

Variations in Blue and Green, c. 1868
Oil on millboard mounted on panel
46.9 x 61.8 cm (18½ x 24⅜ in.), 03.178

Pomegranate, Box 808022, Petaluma, CA 94975

James McNeill Whistler (1834–1903)

The White Symphony: Three Girls, c. 1868
Oil on millboard mounted on panel
46.4 x 61.6 cm (18¼ x 24¼ in.), 02.138

Pomegranate, Box 808022, Petaluma CA 94975

James McNeill Whistler (1834–1903)

Venus, c. 1868
Oil on millboard mounted on panel
61.9 x 45.6 cm (24⅜ x 18 in.), 03.175

Pomegranate, Box 808022, Petaluma, CA 94975

James McNeill Whistler (1834–1903)

Caprice in Purple and Gold: The Golden Screen, 1864
Oil on panel
50.2 x 68.7 cm (19¾ x 27¹/₁₆ in.), 04.75

Pomegranate, Box 808022, Petaluma, CA 94975

Freer Gallery of Art, Smithsonian Institution